BILLY AND
THE WAMPUS CAT

BILLY AND
THE WAMPUS CAT

by

Conrad Reichert

XULON PRESS

Xulon Press
2301 Lucien Way #415
Maitland, FL 32751
407.339.4217
www.xulonpress.com

© 2020 by Conrad Reichert

Printed in the United States of America.

ISBN-13: 978-1-305-0727-5

CONTENTS

MOVING 100 YEARS
TO THE SOUTH

Billy Engel was ten years old when his parents moved away from city life in northern Illinois to a farm in Southern Indiana. In his new community there were nearby towns with weird names like Gnaw Bone, Stone Head, and Bean Blossom. This was the land that time had forgotten. Electric power lines had not yet come into the rural areas of this part of the state, so people who lived on farms did not have electricity.

Billy now found himself in a world of no electric lights, no refrigerators, no bathrooms, no plumbing, no warm furnaces, and no washing machines. This meant having kerosene lamps in the house, kerosene lanterns out in the barn, outhouses, a cold house in the winter and a hot house in the summer, cooking and heating with wood burning stoves, doing the laundry on a washboard or in the creek, and doing special things with foods so they wouldn't spoil. To keep something cool that was perishable, his mother had to wrap it up in a container and lower it down into the well on a rope, where the air was cooler than up at ground level.

The nearest town of any size was about twenty miles away. Each family made up its own police and fire department. If someone had a house fire there was nothing that could be done except to pump buckets of water from the well to throw on the flames, and hopefully to carry some of the valuables out of the house.

On the other hand, this was the safest and most crime free place anyone could ever live. The house was located a half mile back off the county road, and the dogs would let you know long before anyone got near the house. If someone in the family went over to a neighbor's place after dark, they had to do a lot of yelling "HELLO" while they were still some distance away, and someone from the house would call out to the dogs and reassure them that all was well. Every house had several loaded guns stacked in the kitchen corner, and one loaded pistol was on the floor under the father's bed. There was an old saying, "If it ain't loaded, it ain't no gun," so they were all loaded.

Most of the farm homes sat on foundations of large flat stones under each corner of the house, with the stones holding the house up about two feet above the ground. The dogs slept under the house, which was a great vantage point for them because they could see or hear everything going on in all directions. Being elevated on these stones kept the house cooler in hot weather, since a breeze continually blew under the house. No one needed a regular dog house, because the dogs lived under the house. In fact, dogs were accepted as part of the family and they all had their responsibities. They kept away burglars, noticed anything unusual going on and sounded the alarm, helped herd the animals, went hunting with the family, killed rats and other pests that came anywhere near the house, babysat small children, and generally gave everyone a lot of wet kisses.

A creek ran through the field between the house and the county road. Billy knew what it meant when people said, "See

2

you later, Lord willin', and the crick don't rise." It only took a sprinkle and the creek would rise. If there was a good rain, no one was going anywhere for a couple of days, because the water would be running over the roads in all of the low areas. The house itself was up on a hill, and when the creek came up it didn't bother the house. Some of the other neighbors lived on flat land, and when the creek rose, they had about four inches of water running across their yard. Even though their well was under all that water, it didn't stop them from going out to the well and pumping a bucket of water for the house. Yes, the water in the bucket was muddy.

THE ENGEL PLACE

The Engels got their drinking water from a spring a quarter mile away. It was Billy's job to haul water for the house. The spring was up on a hillside, higher up than the high-water level went. It seemed senseless to Billy that when the creek was overflowing, he had to wade in water up to his knees to go get water from up on the hill. Once he got the water, he had to wade back through all that water to get back to the house. It would be so easy to just dip the bucket into the swirling water in which he was walking. But there were rules on what water to drink and what water to not drink. If he brought back a bucket of water discolored with mud, his mother would have him carry several additional buckets before he was allowed to quit. "Funny thing," he thought, "how mothers can read your mind."

Thankfully there was a secondary source of water in addition to the spring, but it was not fit to be drunk by humans. This was water that drained off the roof when it rained, and was used for washing clothes and taking a bath. Women liked to wash their hair with it and said it really made their hair shine. When the builders made the Engel house, they constructed an underground cement tank, called a cistern, that caught rain water draining off of the roof. Then they ran a pipe from the cistern up to a hand pump located above ground, along the side of the house, which made it easy to get to the water.

The roofing on the house was made of cedar shingles with moss growing on it, and if anyone ever thought to take a drink from the cistern, just one sip would send them right straight to the outhouse.

After all the furniture had been brought into the house, Billy asked his mom if he could ride his bicycle up to Gnaw Bone and look around. She said, "Go ahead, but get back before sundown." He took off like a rocket because he wanted to do a lot of looking when he got there.

When he rolled up to the store, he parked his bike and stepped up onto the cement porch, which had an interesting bench you could sit on. There were a couple of old-timers sitting on the bench, but the bench was good-sized and had plenty of room for him to sit down, so he sat down next to the old-timers.

One of the old-timers asked, "Are you one of the family that just moved in down south of here?" Billy said, "Yes." The old-timer asked again, "Do you live down by them tall trees?" Billy answered, "Yeah." "You better watch out if you go back into them trees, 'cause they's a Wampus Cat back there."

Billy tried to get a description of this animal, but the old-timers were really confused about it. When he asked them a question about it, they just mumbled. He asked, "Is it like a cat?" "Mumble." "Does it have fur?" "Mumble." "Have you ever seen one?" "Mumble." "Will it come after you?" "YES!" There was no mumbling about the word "YES."

Whatever it was, Billy didn't want to run into one on a dark night. If he saw one in the daytime he would run away as fast as he could go. But, if he ran into one on a dark night,...

He wanted to see one, but he didn't want to see one.

But the day would come when his worst fears were realized.

GNAW BONE, INDIANA

B illy's home was on a farm just south of the village of Gnaw Bone, in an area of hills and valleys, winding roads and creeks, with several families still living in log cabins.

GNAW BONE, INDIANA   TOWN

People in the area made a living any way they could. One of the neighboring families made their living by digging up sassafras roots, peeling the bark off the roots, and selling the bark to the local stores. People could take a handful of this dry bark and boil it in water and make a flavorful tea. Sassafras tea was a popular drink that tasted good and also cured whatever ailed you. It had a pleasant taste, like root beer soda. Everyone knew when someone from this family was around, because they smelled like root beer. However, this was not any worse than everyone else smelling like horses or cows, which is what everyone else smelled like after they did the morning and evening chores.

It was Billy's job to walk out to the mailbox every day and bring in the mail. It was about a half mile walk out to the mailbox, which was located out alongside the county road. On one particular day, in the middle of winter, when the temperature was well below freezing, while going out to get the mail, he came on a dead deer that was lying on the ground, frozen solid. He couldn't find any marks on it like it had been killed by dogs or by gunshot. However, it had a nice set of antlers that he thought would look great hanging on a wall. So, he went on ahead out to the mailbox and collected the mail, and headed back to the house. He took the mail into the house and gave it to his mother, and then went back outside to the tool shed and got a hacksaw.

At the tool shed, his dad and Mr. Jones, the sassafras man, were talking and smoking cigarettes. His dad wanted to know what he was going to do with a hacksaw. Billy described what he had run into out in the field, and said he wanted to go back and get those antlers because they were large and good looking. The two men had a discussion about this, and figured that since there were no marks on the animal, that probably a pack of dogs had originally been chasing the deer, and that it had finally eluded them, but subsequently died of exhaustion. After the men concluded their opinions on what the animal was doing there, Billy went on with his mission. He used the saw to cut the antlers off and came on back to the house with his prize. After he showed the antlers to everyone, he took them out to the summer kitchen and put them up out of the way. They could stay there until they dried out.

The next day when he went out to the mailbox he went by the place where the deer had been, but it was gone. There was nothing there but the two front and the two back legs from the knees down. There were human tracks in the snow, but no animal tracks. "You don't suppose," he thought, "and why not? It was good frozen venison."

MUD BOG

Saturday night was going-to-town-for-supplies-night after the chores were done. The lane was a half-mile long and if there had been a good rain in the last couple of days, getting the car out to the graveled county road was going to be a major event. It was going to be "do or die!" Laid out between the house and the county road was a half-mile long Mud Bog. The men-folk would have to push the car, with its wheels spinning and mud flying, until the tires could get a good hold. While pushing, they didn't dare let the car stop, or they were in trouble. If the car got completely stuck, they would have to leave the car there and everyone would have to walk back to the house in the mud.

Men walked in mud all the time, but women generally didn't like this because they wore fancy shoes and clothes. Sometimes it got to be late in the day by the time they got the car out of the mud, and the stores were going to be closed by the time they got to town. There was nothing that could be done about it, so, they just called it a day and went back to the house.

On the next day they would go back out to where the car was sitting in the mud, and pull it to solid ground with the horses. The Engels had a tractor, but they also needed horses for pulling the tractor out of the mud when it got stuck, which was often.

Sometimes when the car got stuck the men left the women in the car and walked back to the barn in the mud, and got the horses and wagon, and returned for the women, so they could ride back to the house on the wagon.

All of these goings-on were usually in the dark, since chores had to be done before anybody could leave the place. On the evenings that the family intended on going to town, the horses were not turned out to pasture after the chores were done. They were left tied up in their stalls, just in case they were going to be needed.

At those times when the family was lucky enough to get the car all the way out to the end of the lane, the last hundred yards heard a lot of screaming by the women, and, "Come on Baby. Come on Baby. Come on Baby," by Mr. Engel. And, finally, Halleluiah! "Oh, When those saints! Oh, When those saints! Oh, When those saints go marching in!"

When they climbed out of the car at the county courthouse, they could be tracked halfway across town by the clods of mud coming off of their shoes. City folk sniffed and looked down their noses at the family as they went by. *They* had sidewalks. The Engels were too busy thanking the Lord that they had gotten into town to pay them any mind.

Nowadays young people have "Mud Bog" races. They *deliberately* drive their cars through mud for the fun of it. The old-timers who lived back then wouldn't have known what to think of this. But one thing they would have noticed, these drivers are not wearing their Saturday-night-going-to-town clothes.

SATURDAY-NIGHT-
GOING-TO-TOWN

Eventually, the Engles would make it into town. The courthouse filled the entire block. All four streets that ringed the courthouse were lined with saloons. The county jail was a part of the courthouse, and on Saturday nights when the family came into town there was a steady stream of patrons being escorted across the street to the jail. Billy's mother rushed the kids through this neighborhood, telling them to keep looking straight ahead so they wouldn't look on the face of Satan. The kids were terrified at the thought of looking into the face of Satan, and no one dared look to the side.

COUNTY COURTHOUSE

The Salvation Army band would be in the middle of all this, playing *Bringing in the Sheaves,* and it made Billy want to march by the beat of the big base drum, "Bringing in the sheaves, Bringing in the sheaves, We shall come rejoicing, Bringing in the sheaves!"

When Billy lived with Gram and Gramp in Illinois, he was downtown with Gram one Saturday night, and the Salvation Army band was playing on the street corner where they were waiting for the bus. Billy told Gram he wanted to join the Salvation Army and play the big bass drum. She said "Ve'll see ven yoou grow awp." Gram and Gramp had come from Sweden, which everybody could tell when they talked.

WE HAD TO GO
UP TO MARS

The Engles went into town to get groceries and supplies on the first Saturday night after they moved to Gnaw Bone. After getting groceries, Billy's mom went into a dry goods store to buy a piece of lace material for her sewing.

When she showed the sales lady a sample of the lace she wanted, the sales lady said, "We don't have any of that here. You'll have to go up to Mars to get that."

Mrs. Engel, surprised at having to go to Mars, said, "Pardon me?"

The sales lady repeated herself, "You'll have to go up to Mars."

Mrs. Engel, not quite understanding the clerk, asked, "What do you mean I'll have to go up to Mars?"

The sales lady, beginning to get impatient, said a little louder, "It's just up Washington Street."

Mrs. Engel was getting more confused, and asked one more time, "Whaaat? I don't understand. How can Mars be just up the street?"

Then, spelling slowly, and in a loud voice, the sales lady said, **"M—E—Y—E—R—S! MARS!"**

DRY GOODS STORE, 1944   **CURRENT DRY GOODS STORE**

CURRENT M-E-Y-E-R-S, MARS!

Did you ever notice how people speak to you when they think you are intellectually challenged?

YE HAVE A VEEL HAVE YE

The Engels now lived in a German farming community in which most people had either been born in "The Old Country," or were of the first generation born in this country. This was a community in which time had stood still because of its isolation. After settling into their new home, they paid a social call on the Pfaffenbergers, who lived on the next farm south of them. It was October, and the weather was beginning to get chilly. Everyone gathered around the heating stove and introduced their self all around. Every now and then Mr. Pfaffenberger got out of his chair and went to the stove, opened the door, and spit tobacco juice into the fire. Mrs. Pfaffenberger would say, "Oh, Vill!" and frown in disapproval.

Later, she invited Billy to come out to the kitchen with her and get some cookies. While they were in the kitchen, she asked, "Ye have a veel, have ye?" In Billy's mind he was looking at a wheel, then at everything that had wheels, wondering, "What do I, personally, have to do with a wheel?" Again, louder, in case he hadn't heard, "Ye have a veel, have ye?" Billy's mind was spinning, "Aaaaaah, I don't know," shrugging his shoulders and wondering why he was so stupid.

"You know, you get on it."

He now pictured himself sitting on a wheel, astraddle of it like it was a horse, then sitting on it sideways, and wondering, "Why would I want to sit on a wheel???"

"You know, it has pedals."

("AHA!!! A bike!") "Oh, yeah, I have a wheel."

"They sure are nice to get around on," she said, as she picked up a platter of cookies and headed back into the parlor with cookies for everyone.

The Pfaffenbergers gave the Engels a summary description of all the neighbors, what kind of people they were, what kind of farming they did, and whatever gossip was available that pertained to them. They also offered their assistance in case the Engels had any needs in getting their own farming operation under way.

FORBIDDEN WOODS

The Engels lived a half mile back off the county road. The fields were open between them and the road, and in the back of their house there was about a quarter mile of open fields. Farther back than that it was increasingly wooded, and the farther you went into the woods the darker and denser it got. If there ever was a "deep woods" that was it. No telling what lived back there.

There was a large creek back there with steep sides. In pioneer times a bridge had been built over the creek to make it possible to get wagons and farm machinery across. But it was said that Gus Abend, who lived back in the deep woods, tore the bridge down and cut up the metal parts and sold them for scrap. Scrap metal could be sold for a lot of money. The old pioneer trail was still used by farmers to go cross-country with their animals, since the animals didn't mind walking through the creek. But if you needed to get wagons or machines over to the other side you couldn't cross at this location anymore. You would have to follow the county road for two-and-a-half miles downstream to another bridge where you could cross over. Two-and-a-half miles downstream, and two-and-a-half miles back upstream added a lot of extra distance to your trip, but nothing was ever done to replace the bridge.

There was something mysterious about the woods. Billy's best friend, Lawrence, lived on the other side of the Big Creek. One day when Billy was over at Lawrence's house, his mother warned the boys to never go upstream into the deepest part of the woods. She didn't tell them why, but it was scary to know that there was something forbidden back there. What might it be? Was it human? Was it an animal? Was it quicksand? Was it a mysterious creature that no one had ever seen, but which they knew to live back there?

DEEP WOODS   **ENGEL FAMILY TREE**

There was a big problem about the forbidden woods. There was a place in the creek back there that was called "The Turtle Hole," where the creek was deeper than at other places, and where it was always deep enough for swimming in the summertime when the water level was low elsewhere. Billy and his friends used to fish and swim back there, but they had to keep an eye open for "**The Thing**," just in case. It was scary, but that's where the good swimming and fishing was.

HILLSIDE SCHOOL

Billy went to school in a little one room school perched on the side of a hill. One school teacher taught all eight grades. Two students shared each desk, and often the two were not in the same grade. For example, a fifth grader might be sharing a desk with a sixth grader. The desks were a little wider than standard desks, so everyone was able to get all of their books and papers into their own half of the desk. There was an hour for recess in the morning, an hour for recess in the afternoon, and two hours for lunch. What is remarkable about this program is that when the students graduated from the eighth grade and went to high school in town, they knew just as much as the city kids. One reason for this is that everyone in the room heard and saw everything else that was being taught in all of the other grades. Billy was in the fifth grade, and when sixth grade spelling was being taught, he heard all of their words. So, when he got to the sixth grade, he already knew all of their words. The same thing happened for all of the other classes. Everyone learned everything at the same time, and continued to relearn it every year thereafter.

Families doing homeschooling have discovered the advantages of age-old methods of teaching such as the above, and research indicates that home schooled children frequently perform better academically than public school children, and that they do as well or better when they go to college.

Hillside School did not have electricity, as was the case with many other country schools. There were two outhouses, one for girls and the other for boys. Drinking water was carried from a pump at the bottom of the hill, and put it in a large clay urn at the back of the schoolroom. There was a wood burning heating stove in the middle of the room, and the boys would draw straws to see who could carry in firewood. When they were carrying in wood the teacher couldn't keep track of them, and this opened up opportunities to fool around outside. Carrying in wood was a lot more fun than arithmetic. The girls drew straws to see who could sweep the floor, and this got them out of classes as well. The water carriers also drew straws to see who could go out and fool around. You would be surprised at how much time you can waste bringing in firewood, carrying drinking water, and sweeping the floors. But everybody knew as much as the city kids when they went to high school in town.

On cloudy days when it got too dark for reading, the teacher proclaimed "recess." Classes were suspended and the kids played "Cyphers." This was a game at the blackboard involving making as many Figure Ones as a student could make in one minute. The champion cypher maker in each grade was obtained, and then one grade competed against another until the school champion was finally obtained. There were about thirty kids in the school, so this took up quite a while as the students waited for the school bus.

One day the county health department came to Hillside School and brought a generator that was run by a gasoline motor, which generated enough electric power to run a movie projector. They showed a film about how to know if someone had head lice, and what to do about it. As far as the students at Hillside were concerned, no one around here had head lice. That was something city kids had.

High water was a problem when it rained hard. The creeks came up fast in all the low areas on the road, and there were a lot of low areas that the school bus had to go through to get everyone home. Some of the kids walked to school, but most kids came from about a five-mile radius around the school. Those students who walked to school followed the high ground to get home. Consequently, when there was a thunderstorm the school bus came and got everyone out of there before the water came up. During the day if the bus driver heard by the radio that there was going to be a storm, the driver came to the school to pick up the kids before the storm hit. If it rained heavily during the night, people only had to look out their window at home to see if there was going to be school that day. If the creek was up, there would be no school today.

HILLSIDE SCHOOL, CLASS OF 1948

LAWRENCE'S FATHER

L awrence was Billy's best friend. His family lived on the farm on the other side of the "Big Creek." There was about a mile of woods between their two homes, and the Big Creek ran through the middle of it. This wasn't just a lazy creek. This was a creek with a bad temper. Most of the time it didn't hold any more than two or three feet of water, but the banks rose up about fifteen feet on each side.

The boys knew what it meant when people said, "See y'all later, Lord willin' and the crick don't rise." After a heavy rain the creek would overrun and spill out for a half-mile on either side of its banks. There was a creek somewhere in all that water, but it couldn't be seen because it was under water. No cars were able to travel the roads during high water times, because the roads would be under water in all the low areas. If anyone tried to get through, they might get stranded on a stretch of high ground and be trapped there for a day or two until the water went down.

One day Lawrence came over to Billy's house to do all the things that boys like to do. They went up in the hayloft and jumped in the hay. Then they swung on the ropes that pull the hay up into the loft and played Tarzan, complete with Tarzan's yell. They had to stop Tarzan's yell because it scared the horses, who started kicking the sides of their stalls. They left the barn and went forth on an expedition up the hill from the house, to a ditch where the early settlers used to throw their trash. They found a couple of worn out wooden shoes and put them on and walked around, seeing who could clop the loudest. They were having so much fun that they didn't notice that it was starting to get dark, even though it was too early to get dark. When it started cooling down, the boys began to smell rain in the air. They got the notion that it would be a good idea to start heading toward the barn. They walked at first, and then ran full speed when lightening began to strike.

The rain came down in sheets. At first it was a lot of fun to stand in the barn and look out the doors at the water coming down. Billy's dad came in from the field. "You can't work in this kind of weather," he said, and started busying himself with things that needed to be done in the barn. The small creek down the hill from the house started to spill over its banks, which meant that the house was soon going to be surrounded by water. The house was safe up on its hill, but how was Lawrence going to get home?

The water in the woods was too deep to try to get over the creek. The nearest bridge over the creek was two-and-a-half miles away, but even if Billy's dad had been able to get a car or truck out to the county road, he wouldn't have been able to go anywhere because the water would be running over the roads in all of the valleys. Telephone service hadn't yet been installed in areas back away from the major highways, so Lawrence wasn't able to call home and explain that he was marooned at the Engel place. He wouldn't be able to go home until the water went down.

Darkness was coming and nothing could be done to get Lawrence home, and the rain continued to pour.

Late that night, after everyone had gone to bed, someone was outside pounding on the door. It was Lawrence's dad, coming to see if his son was all right. Mr. Doyle had come through sheets of rain, finding his way by kerosene lantern, wading for a mile through a dark, flooded forest, climbing on floating logs to get over the creek, at great danger to himself, to see if his son was safe. "Was Lawrence still here? Had he left to try to get home? If he did, we haven't seen him!" The boys were sleeping in Billy's room up in the attic and were awakened to hear the men shouting over the sound of the pounding rain. The Engel house had a tin roof, and when it rained things got really noisy. Billy's dad shouted that Lawrence was still here, and did Mr. Doyle want to stay the night, since it was too dangerous to go back through where he just been? But there was a mother back at the Doyle place, knowing not what, and Mr. Doyle shouted that he needed to go back and tell Mom that everything was all right. Mr. Engel shouted "Ok! Lawrence can stay here until the water goes down and we'll bring him home in the car!" Mr. Doyle left, and the boys watched through the attic window, the lantern getting dimmer and dimmer in the rain until it could no longer be seen.

Mr. Doyle had risked his life to make sure that his son was safe.

AUNT MARTHA LOOKS FOR RURAL ROUTE 8

The Engels lived on "Rural Route 8." Don't ever stop someone and ask where Rural Route 8 is, because they won't know, even if they are standing right on it. No one can tell where Rt. 8 is except the mail delivery person. There is no relationship between "Rt. 8" and the actual spot where someone's house sits. When someone says they live on "Rt. 8," it still doesn't tell anyone where they live. Rt. 8 includes all national highways, all state highways, all paved roads, all gravel roads, and all just plain dirt roads that run through a certain part of a county.

One day Aunt Martha decided to come and visit the Engels without telling anyone ahead of time that she was arriving. She loved to pull off surprises on other people, and this was going to be a lot of fun for her. She lived 300 miles away in Illinois, and she was going to come by railroad. Her husband worked for the Burlington Railroad and he could get her a free pass to ride anywhere she wanted.

The nearest she could get to the Engel place by train was twenty miles away in a town where they had a train station. She was a City Person and had no idea what "Rt. 8" meant. When you live in the city finding someone's home is easy if you have their mailing address. You just ask a person where such-and-such a street is, you go there, and you look up and down the street until you find the house with the number on it that you want. Was she in for a surprise.

When she got off the train she asked the first person she saw where Route 8 was. "Rt. 8 is *everywhere*," he told her, pointing north, south, east, and west of the point where she was standing. She asked, "Do you know the Engel family?" "No, I never heerd tell of 'em, Ma'am." She suddenly felt weak in the knees. Her prank was rapidly losing its fun.

There were no telephones out where the Engels lived, so there was no way for her to call and tell them that she was here in town. She spied the county courthouse just across the street from the train station. It was a large building with a lawn all the way around it, and it took up the whole block. There were benches placed here and there on the lawn where people could sit down for a spell and watch the world go by. She picked up her suitcase and crossed over the street and sat down on one of the benches, thinking to herself, "What on earth have I gotten myself into?"

Meanwhile, out at the farm, Billy's dad had just broken one of the drive shafts on the hay baler, which needed to be running non-stop around the clock until all the hay was in. As everyone knows, "You have to make hay while the sun shines." Working at top speed he got the shaft off of the machine and yelled in the direction of the house, "I'm going to town to get this welded!"

Aunt Martha was sitting on her bench and getting more anxious by the minute. Here she was, 300 miles from home and no one knew she was there. "What if a robber comes along? What will I do if he grabs me?" she thought. She decided she would scream at the top of her lungs. "If only a policeman would come by," kept running through her mind. Finally, she decided what she was going to do. She looked in her purse to see if her railroad pass was still there. It was. She was going to go right back across the street and get on the next train going north no matter where it went, and keep on riding trains until one got her to her own hometown. Her free pass was going to get a good workout. She felt safer sitting on a train than sitting on a park bench in a strange town.

As she was going across the street to the train station a black Studebaker was coming along at a good clip, and as it went by her the driver thought, "Boy, did that ever look like Martha," as he hurried on up the street. As the Studebaker went by Martha thought, "That guy sure looked like Bill Engel," and she continued on across the street. As Bill Engel pulled in at the welding shop he thought, "You don't suppose . . . ? No, that couldn't have been her. But, you don't suppose . . . ? I'd better go back there and take a look at her again. But what would she be doing in Indiana?"

Back in front of the train station Martha was still thinking, "That guy sure looked like Bill Engel." She stopped short of stepping up into the station, turned to the right, and hurriedly followed the sidewalk, thinking, "If I look around the corner I might be able to see him turning in somewhere." She didn't know whether he had a Studebaker or not, but by some slim chance, who knows?

The black Studebaker and Aunt Martha each rounded the corner at the same time, headed for each other. "It **is** him!" "It **is** her!" "Oh, Joy!" shouted Martha. It was a loud reunion with several repeats of "Am I glad to see you!" and "What in the world are you doing here?" Two hours later when Bill pulled up to the house there was another loud family reunion with repetitions of, "What in the world are you doing here?" and, "Am I ever glad to be here!"

Moral: you might have the mailing address of someone who lives out in the country, but if it's a Rural Route address, that doesn't mean you will ever be able to find them.

THE DEADLY VIPER

In addition to dairy products, the Engel farm produced a substantial amount of corn and wheat. These two grains have different growth rates, and are planted and harvested during two different times of the year. A farmer can make maximum use of the land he has available, if he plants the two of them in the same field, during the same year. To do this, he uses a complicated planting and harvesting technique. He plants the corn first, in the spring, and allows it to *almost* mature. Then, he cuts the standing corn stalks down in about October, leaving the ears of corn attached to the stalks, and he stacks the cornstalks vertically in clusters, called "shocks," out in the field, out of the way. Then he works up the ground all around the corn shocks with a disking tool to loosen it, and plants winter wheat in the loosened soil.

In the same field, there is corn, stacked up in individual shocks to dry, plus a new crop of wheat that is beginning to grow before the snow falls. The wheat will be about four to six inches tall by Christmas, and ready to be harvested by the next August.

At corn harvesting time, all the neighboring farmers worked together to get everyone's corn crop harvested. One person in the community owned a Corn Shredding Machine, and went from farm to farm with the machine, and all of the farmers in the neighborhood went from place to place, helping to bring the shocks of corn in to the barn lot, where the machine was waiting to be fed.

(This was a common planting and harvesting process used by the Engels and other farmers in the surrounding area during the years when Billy was growing up.

This method of farming came to an end when corn picking machines and wheat combines became available. It was an end of an era.)

The shredding machine picked the ears of corn out of the stalks, took the husks off, and dropped the ears into a wagon that was parked nearby. It then chopped up the corn stalks and blew them up into the hay mow to be used for feed and bedding. Fodder didn't have much food value, but it got one's animals through the winter after the hay ran out.

One day, when the shredder was at the Engel place, the horses and men had been working a long day, and it looked like they were going to have to work here for one or two more days. With sundown approaching, and having emptied their last load for the day, some of the men began leaving for home with their teams. You could hear them going, the harnesses jingling and the wagons rattling as the horses trotted off. The drivers sat on the side of their wagon beds, resting and chatting with the men who were hitching a ride toward their own homes. No one needed to tell the horses where to go. They always knew where home was, even in the dark.

It was dark by the time the last of the wagons came in from the field and unloaded, and some of the men stayed at the Engel place for supper before they headed for home. The wife and kids back at their place would take care of the chores now that it was corn-shredding time. The men had left home with their teams early in the morning, and the family knew they wouldn't be back until after dark, too late for the men to undertake the milking and feeding.

It was now after supper and the men were sitting at the table, lighting their pipes and cigarettes, and noisily slurping hot coffee from their saucers. The heat coming up through the chimney of the kerosene lamp was hot enough to light a pipe or cigarette, and the lamp was passed around to everyone who needed a light. They had Bull Durham tobacco pouch drawstrings hanging out of the pockets of the bibs of their overalls, along with the leather thong attached to the pocket watch that had been passed on down to them by their daddies.

Billy was sitting in the shadows over in the corner. The farther away you are from the lamp, the darker the room gets.

The lamp eventually returned to the center of the table, and conversation began.

Leaning back in his chair, thumbs hooked through his overall suspenders, Henry began telling about an encounter he had that summer with a Viper.

"Yep, I was on my way to town to get a plug." Town was a country crossroads about three miles from his place where a general store was located. The "plug" was rolled up tobacco leaves hard pressed into a shape about the size of a deck of cards. This could be carried in the pocket for several days and a piece could be bitten off and chewed whenever one took a notion to do so. His cheek was puffed out now and he occasionally got up from the table and went to the heating stove in the sitting room, opened the door, and spit tobacco juice into the fire. "I was walkin' across the Steiner place when all of a sudden I come across this Viper. He was a big'n. He rared right up in the air and struck at me. He spread out his neck the size o' yer hand (Henry extended his hand out over the table so all could see how wide the viper spread out its neck.) He hissed at me and jes kep on strikin'. I reached over and broke me off a horseweed about six-foot-long so's I wouldn't get too close to him, and I poked him in the tail with it. He turned around and **struck** right at the place where I poked him (Henry makes his right thumb and forefinger bite his left arm), and **he done got his own self**. He rolled around and around and around (Henry intertwines his arms, making them roll around and around and around) and he rolled over on his back and died right then and there. He was deader than a doornail."

"I went on in to town and set there (on the liar's bench) and talked a while until it started gettin' late. It's a good piece out to my place and I needed to get going before it got too dark 'cause it's mostly woods out there. I went on by the place where I'd seen the Viper, and there he was, deader than a doornail. He was so dead he'd turned black. He was blacker (slaps his knee) than the Ace of Spades (ends his story with a look of triumph).

Eleven-year-old Billy was sitting on the woodpile over in the corner. He felt slithering fear, hoping both that he would and would not come across a Viper some day. In his mind, "One bite and you'd be a goner. You'd be blacker than the Ace of Spades by sundown. They'd find you lying there. Deader than a doornail."

Later that winter, Billy's gramma in Illinois sent him a nature book. There were all sorts of interesting stories to read during the evening after the chores were done. He'd lie on the floor by the heating stove and read by the light of the kerosene lamp. One chapter in particular caught his attention. He read that chapter word for word, several times. It was about a snake called a hog-nosed snake. How it had a little upturned nose, how it would spread out its neck like a cobra, how it would hiss, how it would strike at an enemy but never touch it, how it would roll over on its back and play dead if it couldn't scare the enemy away, and how it was *not poisonous*. Billy thought, "You don't suppose . . .?"

Spring eventually came and things warmed up. Billy had been thinking about that book all winter. One day, Boy and Viper met. Yes, it had a little upturned nose. Yes, it spread out its neck like a cobra. Yes, it hissed loudly. Thinking, "It sure sounds like what that nature book described. I'd better not put my hand down there. If it's not a hog nosed snake I could be deader than a doornail by sundown." He had a short stick in his hand and he lowered the stick down in front of the snake and moved the stick from side to side. The snake spread out its neck like a cobra. It hissed loudly. It coiled up and struck several times, not making contact with the stick. It rolled over on its back and stayed there. **"It's a hog-nosed snake!!!"**

Spring and summer went by and August rolled around. It was time for threshing wheat. The old growly Fordson tractor had pulled the wheat binder through the field, cutting the wheat close to the ground, gathering it together into sheaves, tying the sheaves up, and kicking them out of the machine onto the ground. The men had come along and picked up the sheaves, stacking them together into shocks, where they would stand in the sun, drying further, waiting for the threshing machine. It was a beautiful sight—hundreds of golden shocks standing in neat rows, waiting to yield their grain.

Just as with the corn shredder, one person in the community owned a threshing machine and went from farm to farm to thresh wheat. The machine sat at the edge of the barn lot and the horses and wagons brought the bundles of wheat in from the field and the men fed them into the machine. The machine shook the grains of wheat out of the stalks and deposited them into a wagon, and a blower inside the machine blew the straw into a large yellow stack on the ground. The straw would be used for bedding for the animals during the winter. But, just like corn fodder, straw had mostly no food value, but during a very hard winter when feed for the cattle and horses ran out, a little bit of straw mixed in with whatever hay you had could keep stomachs going a little longer. The horses did the heaviest physical work of all the animals, so they got the best of the feed that was available.

The workday had begun and the threshing machine was at the Engel place. The men arrived at about sunup with their teams and wagons, and miscellaneous jobs were assigned to anyone who hadn't brought a team with them. As usual there was a need for a large number of pitchers. The pitchers are the men who walk along on the ground and go from shock to shock and throw the bundles of wheat up onto the wagon, where the driver arranges the bundles neatly so the largest load possible can be made. Once they get out into the field the horses know what they are supposed to be doing, so the reins are draped over the front end of the wagon while the driver arranges the wheat, and the horses walk along on their own, going from shock to shock. Once loaded, the driver takes the wagon in to the barn lot where he feeds the bundles into the machine. The pitchers remain out in the field and go on to the next nearest empty wagon and start all over again. There is a steady motion of men, boys, horses, and wagons. Loaded wagons are heading out of the field toward the machine, and unloaded wagons are coming into the field, with the arriving driver looking to see where the nearest group of pitchers is about to top off a load. No scholar had ever told them how to work efficiently. They knew that everyone needs to keep working all the time to get a job done. The boys are expected to work hard, and at the end of the day the men say, "You did a good job today and worked like a man." This is how boys learn to be men. The boys don't complain because they have been taught that work is what life is all about. Besides, two or three inspired boys can pitch wheat up onto a wagon faster than the driver can arrange it, and they can make him beg for mercy as he is going under for the third time.

Billy is one of the pitchers today. The shocks are pushed over on their sides and pulled apart so the sheaves can be picked up individually and pitched up onto the wagon. Field mice who have nested in the shocks are uncovered and they go scurrying off in all directions. Snakes like to work their way into the shocks to dine on the mice, and there is a good crop of fat snakes today, including Vipers. Billy has by this time gotten confident in the harmlessness of the Vipers. Henry is there today, too, with his mules. He likes working with mules more than with horses. He is driving up now to the shock where Billy and two other young pitchers are waiting.

Worlds are about to collide . . .

The shock is pushed over by the pitchers. Mice scurry and snakes slither. Billy leans over and picks up the largest of the Vipers and yells "Hey Henry, look at this!" The snake is writhing and curling around his arm, hissing loudly, spreading out its neck like a cobra, and striking in all directions. Henry yells, "You crazy kid, them's poisonous!" and his yelling is making his mules nervous and they begin to jump around in their harness, trying to see what is going on in back of them. Billy yells back "How about this?" stuffing the Viper down the front of his bib overalls. No one knows who did it, but someone placed a viper up onto the load of wheat, which got Henry's immediate attention. He screamed so loud that he terrified his mules and they took off bucking and galloping across the field, strewing sheaves of wheat as they went. The mules accelerated to maximum speed so fast that Henry was plastered spread-eagled against the back of his wagon, unable to get unplastered until the speed of the mules leveled off. He finally got onto his feet and managed to grab the flying reins and brought the animals to a stop. The pitchers came trotting across the field, picking up the bundles of wheat that had fallen by the wayside. The boys didn't dare laugh openly, but there was a lot of smiling amongst them as they reloaded the wagon. Henry was muttering words the pitchers couldn't make out, except for "crazy" and "kids" and a few other words the boys would never repeat in front of their mothers. The other nearby wagoneers, having seen the whole show, turned their backs, stomped their feet, and slapped their knees, their whole bodies shaking with laughter. They knew all about how Henry liked to taunt the boys and that the boys were now getting a little revenge.

To this day no one knows if Henry was telling a tall tale in the kitchen that night just to scare Billy. Was his snake story made up because he was himself afraid of snakes? Why did he yell so loud when he discovered a snake on his wagon? Whatever the truth, on that day in the wheat field, the score was Dumb Kids = 1, Tall Tale Tellers = 0.

BOTTOMLESS PIT

T here was a mysterious Bottomless Pit in the area. On the road going into town there was a swampy area that covered about ten acres, with a rickety, narrow, one lane bridge crossing over it. Years ago when the bridge was built, the flooring had been made of thick boards laid crossways to the line of traffic, and these boards flopped up and down as a car drove across them. Their flopping made loud banging noises, and the sides of the bridge would sway back and forth like they were going to collapse inward onto the car. Just going across the bridge was scary enough, but to know that this was a **bottomless pit** gave the occupants of the car something more to think about.

The way Billy heard about it was that years ago, before there were farm tractors that looked like what we see today out on the farm, there were large steam engines that were used in farming. These steam engines looked just like railroad locomotives—big, black, noisy, long, and with clouds of smoke coming out of their smoke stack. As the story went, a man was driving a large steam engine across the county to get to a job he had arranged to do. Steam engines usually stayed off paved roads because their wheels had steel cleats that dug up the pavement. When he came to what was about to be called the Bottomless Pit, he had a choice—to either try to go across the bridge on the roadway, or to go around the pool, out into the fields, and stay off the road. Steam engines traveled very slowly, perhaps one-half mile an hour, and it would take a long time to go around on land.

Unfortunately, the driver decided to go cross on the bridge in order to save the time it would take to go around. When he got on the bridge it was just too much for the old primitive structure. It had not been built for anything like this. There was a terrible noise and the bridge trembled. The next thing anyone knew was that the bridge was gone and there was a loud hissing and bubbling noise coming from the sinking steam engine. Boards were floating on the water and the engine driver was swimming for his life.

CURRENT BOTTOMLESS PIT

According to the legend, numerous attempts were made to salvage the steam engine, but it was said that the bottom of the hole was so deep that they were never able to find either the engine or the bottom.

Billy had a hard time as a ten-year-old picturing a pool that was so deep that there was no bottom to it, but every time he went over that bridge in a car, with its flopping and banging boards and wavering sides, he kept his fingers crossed.

Could there be a place where there is no bottom to the world? Did the water go to China? Was it pouring out the other side?

BLOWING UP THE CHICKEN HOUSE

Billy's dad hated rats. There is just no other way to put this. When you live on a farm you are going to have rats. They are going to be everywhere. They are just wild creatures looking for a meal, but they gnaw holes where you don't want holes, they build nests where you don't want nests, and they clog things up where you don't want things clogged up. They get into the chicken house and carry away baby chickens. They get into everything that is edible, and they can be destructive to keep around. Furthermore, they have a very bad reputation. It is believed that they carried diseases during the Middle Ages in Europe, and wiped out a large piece of civilization. In addition, they come out of hiding when you're working in the barn and they scare the wits out of you, zipping and zooming around your feet. If they get half a chance they will go right up your pants leg and run all over the place inside your clothes, and you don't dare try to grab them through your clothes because if you grab them, they'll bite. You can't do anything about it except jump out of your pants.

Farms usually have a bunch of cats in residence who enjoy catching rats. But in spite of setting traps and keeping a large number of cats, rats sometimes take it upon themselves to get into your house. When they are in your attic and run from one place to another, they make enough noise to scare everyone in the place. Some people say they sound like a herd of elephants running through your attic. Maybe that description is a little much, but one time the Engels had a bunch of rats in the attic, and they did sound like at least a herd of horses. This was war! Mr. Engel picked up a pistol with one hand and a kerosene lamp with the other and headed up the attic stairs. The construction of the attic was not improved to the point that there was a floor up there, so he was teetering and balancing on the ceiling joists with a gun in one hand and a lit kerosene lamp in the other. Meanwhile, the rest of the family cowered in a kitchen corner waiting for either bullets, fire, or Dad to come down through the ceiling. After a while none of those happened, and Dad came back downstairs, mumbling. The mood was set for the next confrontation with rats.

A couple days later Billy was getting the chickens ready for bed, and it was starting to get dark. He collected the final eggs of the afternoon, rinsed and filled the watering containers, and got a couple buckets of chicken feed from the granary. By the time he carried the chicken feed into the chicken house it was dark. Darkness was not a problem, since he knew by heart where everything in the house was, and he could do this with his eyes closed. The feed was dry corn and wheat that was ground up and mixed together, and was called "mash." The feed dispenser was a hopper-type device fixed to the wall. You raised the cover and fastened it up so it would stay open, and you poured in the feed. The feed would fall to the bottom of the hopper where there were openings that allowed the chickens to get at the feed. You could put enough feed into the feeder to last all day long, so you only needed to do this once a day. This was done in the evening so it would be ready for the chickens the first thing in the morning.

Billy came into the chicken house carrying his buckets of feed and lifted up the lid, but he sensed that something was not right down in the feeder. It was dark, so he leaned over the top of the feeder to see if he could see anything down in there. Whatever it was looked like it was boiling. It looked like a mass of "something" boiling down in the feeder. "WOW!" He shot out of there and headed for the house, with chills running up and down his spine. He ran into the kitchen and grabbed a kerosene lantern, put a match to it, and headed back to the chicken house. When he got back to the feeder, he held the lantern up above his head and leaned over the edge. "WOW!" again. It was rats. It looked like millions of rats. They were swarming all over each other. It looked like something boiling. He was out of the shed again. He didn't want them getting on him or running up his pants legs.

Dad was in the kitchen eating supper when Billy ran into the house and blurted out, "There's a million rats in the chicken feeder!" Dad was a serious skeptic and he wasn't paying much attention to Billy, but Billy kept sounding the alarm. Dad slowly got up from the table, grumbling, to go out and show Billy that he didn't know what he was talking about. When they got to the feeder, Billy held up the lantern and the two of them leaned over and peeked in. **"YOW!"** they both yelled and shot out of the chicken house. Once he got over his shock, Dad said, "I've got something to fix them."

The next morning after they had done the chores and eaten breakfast, they went out and looked over the chicken house to see what needed to be done. Billy gave the chickens their water and feed outside so they wouldn't be in the way. Upon inspection, the rats had chewed holes through the floor and walls of the house so they could come and go as they chose. Rat holes ran along the outside walls of the building which indicated that they had tunnels under the building. Tunnels meant that they probably had nests under there too. Dad told Billy to get a shovel and go along the outside walls and plug up the holes so nothing could come out, and to tamp hard on the plugs so they filled the holes tightly. He said to leave two holes unplugged, one hole on each side of the house.

He then went to the tool shed where machinery was kept out of the rain, and cranked up the old Farmall tractor and drove it up to the chicken house, parking it alongside one of the two holes Billy had left open. He then assembled a couple lengths of pipe and pushed one end of the pipe into the exhaust pipe of the tractor, and the other end down into the hole Billy had left open.

At about this time one of Billy's friends came over to see what Billy was doing. Chester was twelve years old and had recently moved into the area from a farm in Kentucky. He smoked cigarettes, chewed tobacco, and knew more swear words than anyone could ever imagine existed. Dad gave the two boys each a stick about the size of a baseball bat, and said, "Stand by that hole on the other side of the house, and when a rat runs out smack him in the head." The boys took their positions and Dad started up the tractor. The exhaust smoke and fumes poured out of the tractor and went down the pipe and into the tunnels under the house. He revved up the engine and let it die down. He revved it up again, higher this time, and let it die down. Rats started to come out where Chester and Billy were standing and they their duty. Dad did more revving up and slowing down, and finally he revved the motor all the way wide open and held it for a couple minutes, and then let it die down.

BOOOOOOOM CRASH TINKLE BANG!!!!

The engine backfired and ignited the fumes under the house and blew the house about two feet up in the air. The windows of the house blew out, boards from the floor flew everywhere, and it snowed chicken feathers for quite some time. Chester jumped about twenty feet away and while he was still sailing in the air he pronounced every curse word he knew.

When the smoke and dust settled down, everyone went around and picked up pieces that they were going to need to patch up the chicken house. The chickens needed to be able to get inside for the night because there were wild animals that came out at night that would love to find a chicken loose.

They must have killed all of the rats that were living under the house because they didn't find any lying around after the explosion. A serious campaign to get rid of rats was begun after that, which used a lot of traps. The cats did their share of work, and, of course, they enjoyed their job.

Again, Billy's dad hated rats."

LIAR'S BENCH

Every small village in Indiana had a general store that sold everything from groceries to farm tools. There was a store like this near Gnaw Bone. This was a gathering place for people who lived within ten miles of the village. The news concerning everyone in the area was discussed, and every family in the neighborhood was thoroughly analyzed. It was a major socializing center for the community. Not only adults, but also young people hung around in the evening after school or work.

The liar's bench was an important fixture of the store and it served the whole community. There was an inside liar's bench and an outside liar's bench, and the two were used according to the weather. The inside bench was located near the wood burning stove and was in use during the winter, and the outside bench was the major place to be in warm weather.

CAPTION 14. FORMER LIAR'S BENCH

The term "liar's" bench identified this piece of furniture as a place where you could hear either truth or fiction, and you would have to separate out for yourself which was which. This was the place where "fish stories" were told. The bench itself was made of a two-inch-thick rough sawn oak plank, supported by kegs at the ends. This was the most solid piece of furniture that ever existed. Old timers sat at this bench and whittled on sticks, and didn't mind whittling on the bench itself. The initials of virtually everyone in the township were carved into every available place.

FLYING MULES

Remember Henry, the man who told the tall tale about the spreading viper? He was at it again. He was sitting on the "liar's bench" at the store one day and told a remarkable story about an incident that had happened to him and his mules. "It was getting toward the end of wheat planting season and I was so busy that I hadn't had time to get everything planted. I still needed to get seed into the ground on that hill north of my house, so one night when there was a full moon, I hitched up my mules and went out there to plant the rest of the crop by moonlight.

I took a load of seed and fertilizer out there on my wagon and set bunches of it at different places where I could refill my planter as I passed by. Then I started making rounds. I had gone around the field a couple times and was going up the steepest part of the hill when along come this bomber." (There was an air force training field nearby where the pilots were practicing with bombers.) "He was low, just barely over the tree tops. I had me one of them flashlights with three batteries in it, and they throw an enormous amount of light. I shined it up at him and it was so bright that I could see the numbers on his plane.

All of a sudden, I thought it was the end of the world. He turned on all of his lights and they were so bright that they blinded me, and I couldn't see a thing. He scared my mules so bad that they took off running just as fast as they could. In my whole life I never rode on anything pulled by animals that was going that fast. They ran straight up the hill and they were going so fast that when they went over the top of the hill the planter kept on going upwards and flew about a hundred feet before it come back down to earth."

Henry acted out all of the events—looking up at the bomber, pointing his three-battery-flashlight, going blind and holding his hands over his eyes, desperately hanging onto the reins as his mules went thundering up the hill, the planter flying into the air with Henry sitting on top of it, and landing hard on the ground when he returned to earth. There was a lot of slapping his knee and pounding his fist into his hand. But his audience just kept on puffing their pipes and spitting tobacco juice as he told this remarkable story.

Then, looking for approval, he said, "If you don't believe me you go on out to my place and go up that hill and you'll see that there ain't no wheat growing where I left the ground." No one got up to go look. They had him figured out.

Billy was one of the pitchers on the corn shredding run in December and he happened to be up on that hill. Henry's story came to mind. The new wheat Henry had planted in October was now about four inches high, and Billy walked over to the spot where Henry had described flying through the air, but there was a healthy growth of wheat there, just like it had been planted perfectly.

So much for Henry's tall tales.

BILLY'S DAD AND SACCHARINE

A visit by the Watkins Man was a special event. He was a traveling peddler who went from farm to farm selling his wares and spreading the news of the families in the community. He knew who had a baby recently, who was sick with what, and all the latest gossip. He had a Model-A Ford panel truck that could travel through fields and creeks as well as it could travel on roads. One day he stopped at the Engel place. Billy and his mother walked out into the field to where he had stopped, and as they approached, the peddler opened the rear door of the truck and spread out his wares so they could see what he was selling. He showed them shoes, boots, gloves, clothing for work and for town, tools, cooking spices, medicines, fresh produce taken in trade, candy, and a hundred other things.

"Ma'am I have something here that your husband would appreciate instead of sugar. It's called saccharine and it comes in these little bitty pills," he said in an enthusiastic voice, shaking the bottle in front of my mother's face so she could see the little pills flying around. He opened the bottle and let Billy's mother peer down inside. Each pill was a little less than an eighth of an inch in diameter. "Each one of them little pills is equal to a teaspoon of sugar. Have your husband drop one of them into his coffee and watch his eyes light up."

That evening when Dad came in from the field, Mother recounted the visit with the huckster man. She showed him the few items she had bought for the kitchen, and then went into the miracle of saccharine, telling him that each one of these little pills was equal in power to a teaspoon of sugar. Billy's dad was a skeptic. He often made pronouncements about the world and all that was in it. His pronouncement about saccharine was, "No little pill like that is the same as a spoonful of sugar." He violently shook several pills out of the bottle and into his coffee cup. He stirred vigorously until he no longer saw little pieces of pills swirling in the current. Raising the cup to his lips, with the family leaning forward to hear his pronouncement, it came as **"Aaaarrrrggghhh!!! Ptooooy, Ptooooy, Cough, Cough, Cough, Choke, Wheeze, Wheeze!!!"** The Watkins Man was right. Dad's eyes did light up. He never touched saccharine again.

BILLY'S DAD
BUILDS A SAWMILL

Billy's dad was gifted in understanding the laws of physics. He understood statics and dynamics, motion, hydraulics, work, and other engineering principles. When he was busy inventing a new tool or machine, the neighbors liked to mock him and tell him, "That'll never work." But "it" always worked, and they would rush out and try to buy a ready-made whatever it was that he had invented.

The Engel place had a large tract of timber. This was forestry that had never been cut. The trees were primarily oak and walnut and worth a lot of money. The family had just moved onto the farm and had not yet developed a crop system to produce income, so they needed to take advantage of whatever resources were available in order to make a living.

They began harvesting timber in the form of logs, which they hauled to town and sold to different industries which cut up logs according to their own specifications. After doing this for a couple of months Mr. Engel said, "What we really need is a sawmill so we can cut logs into lumber, which is worth a lot more money than whole logs."

One day soon after that a couple of trucks pulled onto the Engel place and unloaded several piles of steel machinery that looked like railroad tracks, large steel circular saw blades, pulleys, levers, wheels, belts, and other weird-shaped objects. This was delivered at around sundown, when it's time to do the chores, so there was no time for gawking at whatever it was. The chores always come first.

After the chores, and supper, Dad and Billy went out with a kerosene lantern to look at what was there. Mr. Engel would stand at one point and stare, then move to another point and use his imagination. He stared and used his imagination for about two hours. A kerosene lantern doesn't throw all that much light, but he looked at the piles until a plan began to form. Tomorrow he would pull apart the stacks in the daylight and lay pieces on the ground to form a–something.

He was good at looking at a pile of pieces that had no form and tell you what it could become. The Farm Bureau Association sometimes asked him to come into town and put together whatever it was that was laying on the ground next to their railroad siding, and he would take it on as a challenge. No one could figure out what that pile of machinery was, but Mr. Engel knew.

The father and son got their morning chores done as quickly as they could and went out to the mystery piles. They pulled the piles apart piece-by-piece and placed them where Dad pointed. They did this all day long until they had a structure that looked like it could eventually amount to something, but whatever it was, it was still a mystery to Billy.

They then went to work with a measuring tape and determined the dimensions of an area where a saw mill could do its work. They went walking around to different places on the farm, and found a place on a moderately sloping side of a hill, where someone with a cant hook could roll a log downhill and onto the carriage of a sawmill. (A "cant hook" is a short pole with a steel hook on the end which is used to roll logs that are lying on the ground.)

Next came the source of power. The two went into town to the junk yard and tore the huge eight-cylinder engine out of a wrecked Buick. They also took the transmission so they could regulate the RPM's of the drive shaft in the workings of the mill. The radiator from another wreck was also taken to provide water cooling for the engine.

The complete overhaul of the motor was a major project. Electrical powerlines had not yet come into this part of the country, so everything was done with hand tools, and a lot of elbow grease. What was needed was boring out the cylinders, installing oversize pistons, installing new valves, and repairing or replacing just about everything that moved. Holes in steel were made with hand drills, cuts through metal were made with hack saws. A reasonable person would say that this can not be done without electrical tools, except Billy and Dad were there and they did it.

This was the world without electricity, and this is the way things had to be done. Steel objects were taken into town to a machine shop where they did welding where it was needed. Assembling the mill was the most complicated part of the project. There were numerous belts, pulleys, and cables that had to be arranged in certain ways to make everything work. There was a sawmill in another town and they went there to take a look at it. What they saw made sense of some of the mysteries that still remained, and they eventually put all the pieces together and got the mill up and running.

THE ENGEL SAWMILL

Chainsaws were as yet unknown, so there was a lot of hard work to do with crosscut saws, axes, steel wedges, and sledge hammers.

Privately-owned sawmills were not the big fancy factories we see on the TV documentaries of today. They were muscle demanding SWEATSHOPS. From cutting trees down with crosscut saws, to loading the logs onto trucks, to getting logs off the trucks and onto the saw carriage at the mill, and to carrying lumber and slabs of wood away from the busy saw. It was hard work.

The drive with a truck load of logs from the woods to the mill, going up and down steep curvy roads with sharp turns, was a wild adventure. Have you ever seen trucks used for logging? The cabs are all bashed in from runaway logs. What is left of the cab leaves just enough room for a driver to reach the steering wheel and the pedals. No matter. The cabs were so hot from the engine that the driver stood outside on the running board to keep cool while going up long hills with the truck transmission geared down to low-low gear. Going down a steep hill with a curve at the bottom was another matter. No one stood out on the running boards when going down a steep hill. You needed to be ready to bail out if something went wrong with the brakes or transmission, which happened to someone often enough to keep you on guard.

This work sounds dangerous, and it is if you don't pay attention to what is going on. No one experienced any serious injuries, but they had to watch out for hornet nests. The old timers told the boys that, "Hornets will sting you right between the eyes, so try to cover your face if they come after you." Everyone tried to cover up, but the hornets would get you before you knew what happened. If you saw a woodsman with two black eyes, you knew what had happened.

TORO THE ROOSTER WAS
MEANER THAN THE DEVIL

T oro was a gigantic Rhode Island Red rooster. One word can describe him, and MEAN is that word. He was very large, the largest rooster on the place, and he ruled the barnyard as harshly as any evil king. He flew into a rage whenever he saw another rooster and attacked without mercy, drawing blood with his dagger-like spurs. He constantly patrolled the barnyard looking for trouble, and if he didn't find any, he would start some. All of the other roosters had been so severely attacked that when they saw him out walking his rounds they would run and hide under the farm buildings.

He chased people. He would come up from behind, and attack. He would start low at the ankles, and work himself upward to their back, beating with his wings and stabbing with his spurs. If you were in the barnyard when he was loose, you had to carry a stick to keep him off when he came after you. He was so big that you could feel the ground shake as he came running up behind you. He was so mean that he even chased cars. The neighbors couldn't come over because he stood in the middle of the lane and dared them to come closer. They couldn't get out of their car for fear he would attack them.

Billy got a piece of baling wire about seven feet long and folded a crook on the end of it. The "crook" was shaped like the crook on the end of a shepherd's staff. The shepherd is able to catch a sheep by hooking this crook around the animal's leg. You can catch all kinds of animals with a crook, and that includes roosters. Billy chased Toro for some time before he got close enough to get his snare around Toro's leg. Toro fought like a wildcat and the feathers flew, but Billy was finally able to tie a dog chain around one of Toro's legs and tie the other end to a Farmall tractor that was sitting in the barn yard. He left Billy with scratches, bruises, and puncture wounds by the time he got him tied up.

Toro made numerous attempts to break free, but he was no match for a steel chain. Everyone felt safer with him tied up.

The other roosters had seen the fight between Toro and Billy. When they noticed that their Evil Enemy didn't walk away from the scene of the battle, their curiosity got the best of them and they slowly came out of hiding to investigate. As they approached, all of their senses were on full alert, ready to make a run for it if Toro attacked. They muttered little warning calls to themselves as though they were practicing for the big warning calls they would make if he came after them. Toro lunged at the approaching roosters but when he got to the end of his chain it violently yanked him backwards end-over-end. The roosters made several test approaches, and after a while they figured out where the line was beyond which Toro could not go.

One of the observers, a large White Leghorn rooster who was Toro's major barnyard foe, and who was covered with blood from his last fight with Toro, made a jump at Toro and backed off. He made another jump and backed off. He began to figure out that Toro couldn't chase him beyond a certain point. Toro needed his legs to fight and he couldn't fight with one leg tied to a Farmall. His spurs were useless, and the Leghorn now knew it. What followed was not a pretty sight. The Leghorn took his revenge and dealt several blows with his spurs that drew blood on Toro. All of the other roosters who had been terrorized by Toro now closed in for the kill, and they attacked him from several sides. Billy took pity on him and chased everybody away and untied the chain, and put him in the corncrib to save his life. The other roosters now strutted around the yard, crowing, flapping their wings, and announcing their victory. However, they kept an anxious eye on the corn crib where they could see Toro peeking out through the spaces between the boards. He was taking names.

The next morning at chore time Toro was turned loose along with the others with hopes that he had learned his lesson. He hadn't. He went on the attack just like he always did and bloodied every rooster he came across. He left off dealing with his barnyard enemies and started giving Billy the evil eye. He approached Billy, looking out of the corner of his eye, lowered his head, stretched out his neck as far as he could, and flared out the feathers on his neck. This was a clear sign that a fight was about to start. Fortunately, Billy still had a broom in his hand from working in the chicken house, and he gave Toro a thwack with it to let him know that he was not as big as he thought he was.

Something needed to be done. He was a menace and was probably going to hurt someone or some *thing*. He was just doing what he was supposed to be doing, but he was doing it too hard. It was time to act for safety's sake.

Billy caught him with his wire snare again and put him in a burlap bag, and took him far, far out into the woods, and turned him loose. He had been enclosed in the bag and couldn't see where he had been taken. He was so big and so mean that he would probably beat up anything in the woods that got near him. But Billy felt sad and hoped Toro would be all right out there.

The next day at about noon, wonder of wonders, here came Toro, walking through the high weeds and approaching the barn yard. He was as mean as ever, chasing anything in the barn lot that moved. Something drastic needed to be done. Billy got another burlap bag and put him in it, and took him about a mile away from the house, past the big creek, and out to the edge of the Forbidden Woods. While doing this Billy had to keep an eye out for **The Thing**. He still didn't know what a Wampus Cat was.

There was no way Toro was going to get over the big creek, which would be necessary for him to come back to the barn yard.

Three days passed. Then, wonder of wonders, here he came. He had walked all that way, over a mile, through what was certainly enemy territory for him. There was no telling how he got across the creek. He was too heavy to fly and there was too much water in it for him to wade. But, nevertheless, here he was. This was the last straw. Billy put him in a sack again and walked down the road to a campground where farm workers stayed during the summer, and asked the first person he saw if they wanted a chicken. They did.

THEY'S A FOOL BORN
EVERY MINUTE

The only breeds of milk cows around Gnaw Bone were Jerseys and Guernseys. The Jerseys were a pleasant brown color all over, and the Guernseys were a light brown color with large patches of white. Both breeds gave milk with a high butterfat content. This was a rich tasting milk.

Mr. Engel was an avid reader of the *Prairie Farmer*, a newspaper for farmers that came in the mail. He had been following articles about Holstein milk cows that were popular in Wisconsin. There were no Holsteins around here, so there was no one to go and talk to about their cows. He kept reading in the *Prairie Farmer* about the high volume of milk that Holsteins gave. The Engels were developing a herd of milk cows, and were currently conforming to the Jersey and Guernsey popularity, however, he was still thinking about Holsteins.

One day he decided that he was going to take a truck up to Wisconsin and bring back twenty Holstein heifers and raise them up to milking age, and see if they could be used to make a better income than Jerseys and Guernseys. The neighbors thought this was the biggest joke of the century, and they all said, "Them Holsteins ain't no good fer milkin'. Their milk is as thin as water. Yer just gonna drive all the way up there and throw yer money away. You know what "the man" said. "They's a fool born every minute."

Dad knew what "the man" (P.T. Barnum) said, but he borrowed the money and went anyway.

ENGEL'S HOLSTEINS

About three years later almost all of the farmers around Gnaw Bone went to Wisconsin to buy Holsteins. They had been watching the Engel herd and asking employees at the dairy what amounts of milk the Engels were delivering to the dairy.

It turned out that the butterfat content of the Holsteins was, in fact, thinner than that of Jerseys and Guernseys, but Holsteins gave tons more milk than the Jerseys and Guernseys, and were financially far more productive in the long run.

Moral—Maybe there is a fool born every minute, but every now and then one of them comes up with a bright idea.

WOW! A CHAINSAW!

The Engels cut trees with axes and crosscut saws and could only imagine such a thing as a saw with a motor on it. One day while Dad and Billy were working in the timber, they heard a racket going on a couple miles away and wondered what that noise was. It was a motor noise, but it didn't sound like any motor they had ever heard before. Billy's best buddy, Lawrence, heard it from his place and wondered what it was. He wasn't working that day so he walked cross-country to where the noise was coming from. He told Billy all about it the next time they got together.

Lawrence explained the weird noise, "It was a chainsaw, and man did that thing cut wood! The sawdust just flew!"

Billy wanted more information and asked, "What did it look like?"

Lawrence answered with, "It was a motor and it had a chain on it."

Billy, perplexed, wanted more, "What do you mean a motor?"

Lawrence made another description attempt with, "Like a wash machine motor." Lawrence's mother had a Maytag wash machine powered by a gasoline motor, so Billy got a feeling about the size of the motor. Nowadays we would see this type of motor on a lawnmower. But he couldn't get a grip on the "chain." He handled log chains all day when he was working in the woods, and in his mind's eye he saw a wash machine motor with a log chain on it. He had a hard time picturing how you could cut a tree in two with a log chain. He asked several more questions but Lawrence never got beyond the "wash machine motor with a chain on it." Billy was left to think about that mystery until one day in town at the Sears Roebuck store, he saw one. "WOW! THAT BABY OUGHT TO REALLY CUT WOOD!" He had never gotten on to the idea that Lawrence was not talking about a *log* chain, he was talking about a *bicycle chain with teeth on it.* The Engels later bought a chain saw, and THAT BABY COULD REALLY CUT WOOD!

BULL FIGHT AT THE BOTTOMLESS PIT

The Bottomless Pit is in a swampy area where a steam engine fell in and was never found again. The water was said to be so deep there that when they went to recover the engine, they couldn't find it. In fact, they said it was so deep there that they couldn't even find the bottom.

Billy and Dad had gone into town to get some repair parts for the hay rake, and they were on their way back home. To get the parts they wanted they had to go to a town that was located on the other side of the Bottomless Pit.

They were in the process of coming back across the fearful bridge, with the boards pounding loudly and the side rails swaying back and forth, when **WHOA!** There was a huge Black Angus Bull standing in the middle of the road where it exits off of the bridge. He was facing them with his head down and was snorting and blowing air through his nostrils. Just to emphasize his point, he pawed the ground every now and then like he was going to charge. He was warning them that they were not going to go any further down this road. There were about a half dozen Black Angus cows calmly eating grass along the side of the road. No doubt he was with them, because there was no one else around who looked like him.

71

He seemed to be getting more agitated and he pawed the ground some more, like he was thinking about charging. Billy said, "Dad, blow the horn at him." But, Dad said, "I don't want to blow the horn or race the engine at him, because he might think we are challenging him. If he charges, he will hit the radiator and punch a hole through it and we'll be stuck here until someone comes along who can tow us into town."

They decided to just wait it out and hope that this crowd will wander away after a while. It would be too dangerous to get out of the car and try to chase them away. In the meantime, they were trapped, still on the scary bridge.

There was a radio in the car and Dad turned it on to while away the time while they were waiting. The radio just made the bull mad and he started snorting and pawing again. All they could do was just sit and wait. It seemed like hours before the cows sauntered off to feed somewhere else. With the cows leaving, the bull didn't have any further purpose in keeping Dad and Billy prisoners, so he left too, but he whirled around and looked at them every now and then, just to let them know that they had better not try anything sneaky.

As soon as the bull got off the road and a little distance away, Mr. Engel started the car and took off like a shot. He gave the car horn a bunch of beeps to let the bull know that they were going to come and go whenever they pleased.

AUNT MARTHA AND THE COW FLY

A unt Martha was a City Person. The idea that there could be a place where all kinds of large animals were walking around loose scared her. She walked up to the pasture fence, and the cows being curious, came over to where she was standing and looked at her. She wanted to know if cows bite, and she was assured that they might give her a big wet smooch, but they wouldn't bite. Unfortunately, a cow standing near her went "**MOO**." The world had never before heard such screaming. She took it personally. She felt that anything that made a noise like that had to be dangerous. As far as she was concerned, the moo of a cow was pretty much the same as the roar of a lion. If a cow moos, the next thing that is going to happen is the cow is going to attack.

One day she was watching Billy pumping drinking water for the horses. The horses had been working in the field and were still in their harness, and were standing side by side slurping in the water from the trough. The trough for the horses had been made from a hollow beech log, sawed off at the ends, with boards nailed across the ends so it would hold water. There was a long pipe that went from the pump to the trough, and you would have to give about two hundred pumps on the handle to fill the trough enough to satisfy the horses.

The usual swarm of flies were buzzing around the horses, but there was one fly that was five times bigger than the others. It was a "cow fly." Cow flies aren't particular about whether the animal they dine on is a cow or a horse. They like them both the same. This particular fly didn't care whether he dined on cows, horses, or *people*. He just wanted a meal. He left the horses and came to where Billy and Aunt Martha were standing, and he circled each one of them a few times, and then headed straight for Aunt Martha. He found a spot of bare skin on the back of her shoulder and bored in. **YOOW!!!** In her mind she was sure that she had just been bitten by a cow!!! This was louder than the scream caused by the MOO. She terrified the two horses that had been drinking, and they took off bucking and kicking, and galloping away from the sound of the scream as fast as they could. They were still tied together in their harness, running through the creek, through two barbed wire fences, dragging along several fence posts and a long length of barbed wire, and they finally got tangled up in a jumbled mess of blackberry briars, fence posts, barbed wire, and wild grape vines. They were down on the ground and they couldn't move.

They had taken off so fast that there was no chance to grab the reins, and all anyone could do was run along behind them hoping that neither of them would get hurt. When Billy and his dad finally caught up with them and saw the mess they were in, they ran back to the barn and got axes, saws, and wire cutters so they could cut them out of their entanglement. The horses were scared to death. They rolled their eyes and kicked and screamed as Billy and his dad struggled to free them. They had to start cutting away the vines and barbed wire at a distance away from them so they wouldn't get kicked. It took a long time but they were finally able to cut their way in close to them. Their harness was hopelessly tangled up with them and all of the other debris, and nothing could be done except to cut the leather harness straps along with everything else. The animals were more important than their harness.

They eventually got the horses untangled and up on their feet. They were still scared but Mr. Engel talked to them in his most soothing voice as he felt all over their bodies, looking for cuts and broken bones. Their shins were badly skinned up and there were a few places where they lost patches of hide, but it was a miracle that they didn't have any major injuries. They were treated with hot packs, blue horse medicine, and exercise for the next few days, and they limped around for a while, but they eventually recovered fully.

TAKING A FROG AWAY
FROM A SNAKE

I t had been a hot day all day. The Engels were putting in a new fence line along their east boundary, where they wanted to create a new pasture for their cattle. During the previous winter, when they had been cutting logs for the saw mill, they had set aside thinner logs that were too small to cut up into lumber, but which were just right to become fence posts.

Billy had been digging holes all day, and the new fence posts were going to be set in these holes. It was getting close to quitting time, and he was covered with dirt. When you live on a farm, you spend a lot of time doing things that get you dirty. He knew that his mother would never let him set foot in the house, as dirty as this. But there was a cure for being dirty. It was The Bathtub.

There was a creek down the hill just east of the house, where there was a place the Engels called "The Bathtub." The water at that spot was about eighteen inches deep and you could just sit down in the creek and take a bath. The water came from a spring on the Engel place, so they knew that it was clean. The bed of the creek was gravel, which was continually being washed clean. So, this was a good place to take a bath as long as you didn't mind taking a cold bath.

Billy went to the house and picked up some clean clothes, and then headed for the creek. He was just lounging in the water and letting it run over him, when he heard a splash coming from upstream and around the bend. He froze and listened, waiting for it to happen again, which it did. He continued listening and it happened again a few minutes later. From where he was, he couldn't see what was making the noise, so he rolled over onto his stomach and partly crawled and partly floated upstream in the direction of the sound. He eased himself around the bend and lay still, watching for something to move. There it went again, and this time he saw it. It was a large blacksnake, about six feet long, catching frogs. He had a frog headfirst in his mouth and the frog's legs were running full speed in reverse, trying to back out of the snake's mouth. He watched this scene for a while, but the snake had a good hold, and the frog eventually disappeared all the way.

Billy didn't want to bother the snake because he knew that snakes were good to have on a farm. They eat mice and rats and other pests that you would like to do without. He eased himself back downstream to the bathtub and continued on with his bath.

About two months later he was bringing in the cows for their evening milking. The cows were casually walking along, knowing where they were supposed to be going. They knew that when they got to the barn, they were going to get a snack, and then they were going to give the farmer their milk. This was their job. They were walking along in a single file on a trail that went to the barn, and Billy was walking along behind them, making sure that everyone kept moving. Otherwise, they would dawdle and take forever to get there. All of a sudden, the lead cow lowered her head, kicked, and jumped to the side, and then settled herself back down on the path, continuing along at the usual pace. The cow that had been following her did the same thing. Her head went down, she kicked, she galloped a few steps, and then settled back down. This was at the same spot where the first cow had reacted.

Billy threaded his way through the herd until he got to the spot and looked around. Wow! It was a large blacksnake with frog legs sticking out of its mouth, and the legs were moving at full speed, trying to get away. This was a large snake just like the one he had seen in the bathtub. The creek was about two hundred feet away from where he was standing, and he figured that the snake had been hunting again, and followed the frog out into the pasture. It gave him the chills just thinking about the frog running to get away and the snake slithering along in the grass behind him. He felt pity for the frog.

He reached down with his left hand and grabbed the snake by the neck, and tried pulling on the frog's legs with his other hand. The snake had a good hold on the frog and didn't want to let go, but Billy had angered the snake to the point that he wanted to wrestle with Billy's left arm, and he was all over Billy's arm. Billy wrestled the snake with his left arm, and pulled on the frog's legs with his right hand until, he got the frog out. He dropped the frog to the ground but now he had the snake to contend with. He knew blacksnakes were not poisonous but he also didn't want to get bitten, because they have teeth and they can draw blood. Billy needed to get a better hold on the snake's neck, which he tried to do with his right hand, but the snake was faster than the eye and grabbed onto Billy's right hand. Billy's hair stood right straight up! What a creepy feeling to have the tail of a snake wrapped around your left arm, while the head of the snake is holding your right hand in its teeth. Billy ran around in circles trying to shake him off.

Eventually the snake let go, and Billy stopped running. He checked his hand, and found that the snake had left bloody teeth marks on it, but no major damage was done other than that.

Billy went back to check on the frog, who was staggering around trying to figure out what had just happened, and the upper half of his body, which had been inside the snake's mouth, was not as dark green as his legs. It was almost as though the green got sucked out of him. The frog then went one way, the snake went another, and Billy went the third way, straight ahead with the cows to the barn.

Sometimes it doesn't pay to get too helpful with nature.

SNIPE HUNTING

O ne day one of the older boys asked Billy if he knew what a "snipe" was. Billy told him that he had never seen one, and asked, "Are they a bird?" The boy answered, "I can't describe one to you. You have to see one." Billy still didn't know what a Wampus Cat was, so he was being cautious. Still trying to get a recruit, the boy continued, "They are really good eatin', and you don't need a gun to get them. All you need is a gunny sack. All you do is go out in the woods in the dark and hold the mouth of the sack open. They just come right up to you and go right in the sack."

The older boys worked on Billy and his friends until they had a kid talked into going snipe hunting with them. The hunting rules were to get a gunny sack and wait until dark, and then go out to where the snipes hang out. The boys would show you where to wait with your sack open. They would bring a lantern so they could find their way around in the woods.

Billy didn't have to think about this very long. He had no strong need to go into the deep woods after dark. That is where the old timers told him THE THING lived.

But they worked on Clarence Johnson until he said he'd like to go hunting with them the next time they went.

Clarence told Billy all about snipe hunting a couple days later. "You take your gunny sack and go out in the woods after dark, and someone will show you where to wait. The place that the snipes like is the darkest place you can find, and as close to a swamp as you can get, since the snipes like to catch frogs. Don't worry if you get your feet wet, they'll dry off later."

According to the plan, the boys tell you to get your sack ready and they will go out and scare the snipes in your direction, and, oh, they need the lantern to find their way back here again. (The boys leave, but they aren't going to scare any snipes in your direction, they're going to go home. And you're going to sit in the dark, holding the bag, and listening to things swishing around in the water in the swamp.)

Clarence sat in the dark, holding the bag open just like he had been told. A long time passed and the older boys began to wonder if everything was ok. No telling what might happen out there in the swamp. The boys lit a lantern and headed out to find Clarence. But there he was, sitting on a stump, holding his bag open, and waiting for a snipe.

When he had told Billy his story, Billy asked, "Clarence, did you catch any snipes?" "No," he said, "I didn't see ary a one."

This was a popular prank that some people fell for. 'Coon and 'possum hunting were popular sports, and were done at night, which made snipe hunting seem all the more logical to the uninformed.

IT'S THE END OF
THE WORLD !

I t was October. The land plus the Engel family's hard work had produced a good crop of corn that year. The weather was starting to cool down and the leaves on the corn stalks were turning from green to brown. Heavy ears of corn were hanging upside-down on the stalks, no longer able to keep their heads up. Pumpkin seeds had been mixed in with the corn seeds when planting that spring, and hundreds of pumpkins were lying all over the field.

Grass in the pastures was now getting short and it was necessary to start making use of what had been planted that spring. Several wagon loads of pumpkins were brought in and piled up in the barn lot where they would be given to the animals at feeding time. Armloads of corn were also brought in, especially for the horses. However, this was all temporary work, just to get feed to the animals while other things were being done to get ready for the regular harvest.

The next big job was going to be cutting corn and standing it up in shocks out in the field so it could be taken in to the barn area when the corn shredding machine came on its route.

One person owned a corn shredding machine, and took it to all the farms that had raised corn that year. All the farmers would get together and work at each farm, gathering up the shocks of corn that were standing out in the fields, and taking them to the corn shredding machine that was parked in the barn lot. The machine would pick the ears of corn out of the shocks and drop them into a wagon parked next to the machine. It would grind up the empty corn stalks and blow them up into the hay loft for use as bedding for the animals during the winter.

It was now October, and there would be several nights of a bright "harvest moon." The light thrown off by the moon is so bright at this time of the year that you can see to work in the fields at night, so this is a good time for cutting corn.

Cutting corn is hard work. You have to use a long knife so you don't have to bend over so far. A "corn knife" is a long knife that you can make or buy and it looks like a machete.

On this particular night Billy went out to cut corn with Dad for a couple of hours, but he was in sixth grade at school and needed to get to bed before it got too late. Eventually, it started to get close to bed time, and Billy said, "I'm going to head for the house, Dad. I'll see you in the morning." Dad responded with, "Ok," and Billy left.

His dad stayed out there intending to cut corn all night. It got to be about midnight when he thought he saw something out of the corner of his eye. He stopped working and looked all around, but didn't notice anything unusual. So, he went back to work. But there it was again. What was it??? He looked all around, and listened, but nothing happened, so he went back to work. WOW ! ! ! It was stars falling. Not just one or two. **IT WAS MILLIONS ! ! !**

He headed for the house on the run. **WAS IT THE END OF THE WORLD? ? ?** He was not much of a church-goer but he had heard, **"REPENT! THE END IS AT HAND!!!"** And this sure looked like it.

Everyone back at the house was sleeping but it didn't take him long to wake everyone up. More and more stars were coming down all the time. Everyone's knees were shaking. What was there to do? If the Lord was coming right now it was too late to "get right with God." Everyone said their prayers and promised God they would be better persons if He spared their lives.

It was a long night.

When the sun came up the next morning, everyone found that they were still alive, but completely worn out from praying all night. As the new day slowly crept by, their knees stopped shaking and they began to recover normal speech.

Does this sound crazy?

Exactly 55 days before this particular day, a new terrible bomb had been dropped on Japan. It was called **The Atomic Bomb!** The Engels had only just heard about it a couple days ago. People all over the country were afraid about it, and even some scientist were afraid THE BOMB might blow up the whole world.

Just hearing about it and then seeing the heavens falling, the Engels thought it was surely THE END.

Everyone actually did become better persons for the next few days.

It would still be a good idea to end the day with a few moments of meditation, and to promise oneself to be a better person, because . . . you never know.

ELECTRICITY!

When electric power lines came into the Gnaw Bone area it was like the Act of Creation. **"LET THERE BE LIGHT!!!"**

Electric lights came on. Water ran from the faucets. Indoor bathrooms worked. Refrigerators came alive. Radios turned on. Wash machines did the laundry. Toasters made toast. There were electric lights in the barn and outside in the yard. Electric tools and appliances became available to do work for both men and woman.

It was a while before people could comprehend what they could do with electric power, but eventually they learned how to take advantage of this new miracle of energy.

POPPIN' JOHNNY

A "Poppin' Johnny" was a beloved tractor found on many family farms. Its formal name identified it as a John Deere tractor. The "popping" in its name came from the sound of its motor. It had a two-cylinder motor that ran at low RPM's, a low number of revolutions per minute. If you heard a pop-pop-pop-pop-pop-pop sound somewhere in the neighborhood, it was a John Deere tractor. It made about two pops a second.

This tractor was useful for light-to-medium duty farming. Most of its weight was centered over the rear wheels where traction was important. However, it was very light on the front end. You learned this the first time you hooked up to something really heavy. The front end of your tractor would rear up off the ground, and if you didn't release the clutch while it was on its way upward, you could be in a lot of trouble. Not very many tractors went all the way over backwards, but everyone heard of some that did. The tractor would be on top, and the driver would be underneath.

Other than this, it was a popular tractor, tall and green. It would pull a two-bottom plow, except you didn't want to plow while you were going uphill. This got you into the front-end problem. If you were going to try an uphill furrow, something in your head told you to slide over to the edge of the seat just in case you needed to bail out. If you had to plow a furrow in an uphill-downhill direction, you had to turn the tractor around and back it up the hill, and then plow in the downhill direction. The front end would stay down when you did this.

A POPPIN' JOHNNY

If you were "plowing corn," or "cultivating corn," you would encounter another legendary experience with a John Deere. The tractor would put you to sleep. The sound of the motor had a hypnotic effect to it, and driving at the necessary low-low speed, hour after hour, with the hot sun beating down on you, your eyelids would get heavier and heavier and you would suddenly find yourself in the woods with your frontend up against a tree and a hundred yards of barbed wire and fence posts strung out behind you. This happened to everyone who ever worked with a Poppin' Johnny.

There was another experience that many farmers had with this tractor. The Poppin' Johnny was the transitional tractor for many persons who were going from using horses and mules to using tractors. Everyone had the experience of driving the Johnny into a farm shed to park it. When they got it in the shed, they yelled "WHOA" and pulled back on the steering wheel. Of course, this works when you're driving horses, but not when you're driving tractors.

There you are again, with the frontend up against something and broken things lying around.

Some of these folks, to this day, have a tall green tractor sitting out of the way in their garage, next to their fancy modern car, even though they don't live on a farm anymore.

WAMPUS CAT!

According to Billy Engel, somewhere in the area of Gnaw Bone there is a Wampus Cat lurking in the deep woods. No one can describe exactly what it looks like, or what it sounds like, and it only comes out at night, and when it comes out it's only in the deep woods.

As he tells it, "As far as I know I am the only person alive who has had a personal contact with one, and I have the scars to prove it. My encounter happened on a dark night when I was eleven years old.

I first heard about the Wampus Cat from old timers. They would say something like, "You'd better watch out if you go back in them woods. They's a Wampus Cat back there." I would ask them to tell me what it looked like, but no two people ever said the same thing. They seemed to be very confused about it. I asked them if they had ever seen one, but they would just mumble. I'd ask, "Is it like a cat?" "Mumble." "Does it have fur?" "Mumble." "Will it come after you?" "**Yes.**" There was no mumbling about the word "Yes." Whatever it was, I didn't want to run into one on a dark night. If I saw one in the daytime, I would at least be able to make a run for it. But if I ever come across one at night, **sheesh!**"

I wanted to see one, yet, I didn't want to see one.

But the day was coming when my worst fears were realized."

That day came!

On that day, before he left for school, his dad said, "I'm going to be working at the neighbor's place all day and I won't be getting home until late. After you get home from school take care of the chickens right away and then go out to the pasture and bring in the cows and horses. Put them in their stalls and do the evening feeding. I'll take care of the milking when I get home. Give each of the horses six ears of corn, and fill their mangers with hay."

It was autumn now and the pumpkins were ripening out in the fields. Dad and Billy had recently brought in a wagonload of pumpkins and piled them up in the driveway in one of the farm buildings. Pumpkins were like ice cream and cake to the cows. They loved nothing better than to find a chopped-up pumpkin in their feed box. Dad continued on with his instructions, "Give each cow two chopped-up pumpkins and fill their mangers with hay."

"Now, be sure you get them in before **dark**," he said, talking in a louder voice, "because you won't be able to find them after dark if they're out in the woods." Billy replied, "Ok, Dad."

Dad repeated himself again, this time pronouncing every word loudly and clearly, **"BE-SURE-YOU-GET-THEM-IN-BEFORE-DARK."** Billy assured him again that he would. With that, Dad left the house, climbed up on the John Deere, and Put-Put-Putted off toward the neighbor's place, with, "Be sure you get them in before dark," still ringing in Billy's ears.

After finishing breakfast, Billy grabbed his lunch box that Mom had packed, said goodbye to her, and headed out into the day. School was about a mile away, which he had to walk every morning and evening. To get a ride on the school bus you had to live farther than a mile away. The walk to school did not follow the county road, but went as the crow flies, over hills, through valleys, and through a swamp. If he pretended that he was leading an expedition through the jungle, he could make the time go faster. He could also trek through the frozen wastes of the North in the wintertime, or even climb Mount Everest. There were creeping, crawling, flying, and swimming things to look at and to poke at on every expedition."

Today the time at school passed with its usual lessons and events. This was a one-room school, containing all eight grades. The students recited, they read out loud, they wrote on the blackboard. The boys teased the girls, and the girls tattled on the boys. But the educational system survived and it was eventually time to go home.

Billy launched the evening expedition and headed toward the equator in his imaginary jungle, but as he was about half way through the swamp, he jolted to a stop. "What is this?" he wondered. About twenty Canada geese had taken possession of the swamp since he passed this way this morning, and their loud calls made no secret that they were going to stay here for the night. He had seen geese flying over, but they were always up at a high altitude and never down on the ground like this. He got as close as he could in order to get a good look at them, getting his feet wet in the process. He practiced imitating their calls, but they were not impressed. No matter how well he honked, he was only a human being as far as they were concerned, and they stuck their noses up in the air and snubbed him completely.

Time goes by rapidly when you're having a good time, and he was having a good time. The minutes had been ticking away rapidly, when the nagging thought that had been floating around in the back of his mind suddenly erupted into **"BE-SURE-YOU-GET-THEM-IN-BEFORE-DARK!"** "Oh, no!" He moved into high gear, partly running and partly walking, with his water filled shoes squirting and making watery noises. He was breathing hard when he came running into the yard. He didn't even slow down as he went through the house, in through the front door and out through the back, grabbing his barn clothes on the run, and heading straight for the barn. It was starting to get dark!

He filled two pails with chicken feed and headed for the hen house, dumping the mash into the feeders. Three or four trips with buckets full of mash were required to fill the feeders. He refilled the water containers and collected the eggs that had been laid since his mother picked up eggs earlier in the day. The chickens taken care of, he went to the barn and opened the doors on one side of the barn for the horses, and on the other side for the cows. The barn was empty and everyone was outside.

It was October and sundown was occurring earlier and earlier each day. He climbed up on the barn lot fence and peered out over the fields, looking for the animals. He called the horses, but there was no answer. He tried the cows, but it was the same thing. Nothing answered and nothing moved. He strained his eyes and ears for any hint of an animal, but there was nothing out there but gathering darkness. His heart sank. "They must be back in the woods!" he told himself. He hurried to the house and got two kerosene lanterns, lit them, and told his mother that he was going to look for the animals. She had been there when Dad told him to get the animals in before dark, but she didn't say anything about his lateness in getting home from school.

Hurrying toward the barn, he paused just long enough to hang one lantern on a nail on the outside of the barn and the other one just inside the main door. The inside lantern would be necessary for lighting the inside of the barn when he got back with the animals. The outside lantern wouldn't cast light far enough to be any help in finding the cattle, but in the dark it would help him to keep his bearings. Once he found the animals, he could herd them in the direction of the light. He headed straightaway for the woods, since it was almost certain that they were back there. It continued getting darker by the minute. There was some light in the sky and he could see the ground well enough to follow the cattle trail that was winding its way toward the woods. He was familiar with all of the different animal trails and he knew where this one was going.

As he hurried along the trail, he hoped that the horses and cows were all in the same place. If they were not, one group sometimes goes in one direction and another group goes in another direction, and you can't get them all heading toward the barn.

At the edge of the woods, light met its opposite. It was like stepping through a curtain into blackness. If he looked upward he could see the darkened sky up between the treetops, but he could not see straight ahead or to either side. He proceeded slowly into the woods, looking upward to avoid running into trees. "UGH! AAAGH!" He had walked face first through a spider web strung between two trees, and the strands of the web criss-crossed his face and wrapped around his ears. "UGH!" He hoped he didn't have one of those large yellow and black spiders crawling on him someplace. He held one of his arms out in front of himself so he wouldn't get another one in the face as he walked ahead. He stopped every few yards, hoping to hear something. He continued to call, first the cows, and then the horses, but he heard nothing in return. He stood stock-still and sniffed, hoping to get a smell that he recognized, but there was no breeze and smells were not moving around.

It was dark and he couldn't see anything. He didn't know it, but the animals were standing all around him in the dark, being very quiet. They were watching him, but they weren't moving a muscle. One cow had a bell around her neck so she could be found in the dark, but she was standing just as still as everyone else.

Billy could hear his father saying, "BE-SURE-YOU-GET-THEM-IN-BEFORE-DARK." He wondered how he would ever be able to explain this. His father didn't like to hear excuses, and Billy didn't dare go home without the animals. He was thinking,"Maybe I can get the animals into the barn before he comes home, and then act like this never happened."

RRROOOAAARRR!

"WAMPUS CAT!!!" Billy screamed."

The most dreaded thing in life had happened! He had run into a Wampus Cat on a dark night! His feet threw up clods of dirt. Clouds of leaves swirled in his wake as he streaked through the woods, looking upward to try to see where the trees were. He bounced off several trees as he raced along."

RRROOOAAARRR!

He could hear the Cat coming. It sounded big! It was crashing through the brush as it came closer. It was galloping like a monster, and he could feel its hot breath getting closer and closer. It shook the ground as it took each leap.

RRROOOAAARRR!

Never mind that the last roar had a bit of a Holstein accent to it. Billy was concentrating on attaining the speed of sound. As he cleared the edge of the woods he could feel his clothes ripping away and sharp claws tearing his skin, and then—
WOW—FLYING—SUMMERSAULTING—SPLOCK!

When he regained his senses he found that his mouth was full of mud. He was face down in the creek bank. Instantly his arms and legs began rotating like high-speed windmills and he flew up the opposite bank and headed for the light off in the distance. No human being had ever moved this fast. He made it across the open meadow in almost nothing flat and literally flew through the open barn door, leaped over the mangers, and landed in the safe inner sanctum of the barn. A thundering herd of cows and horses came crashing into the barn right behind him, with everyone trying to go through the same door at the same time. Boards were flying everywhere. The horses were where the cows ought to be and cows were where the horses ought to be, and the horses ended up on top of the cows' mangers, with their legs all tangled up in boards.

It took him some time to get everyone calmed down and the horses out of the mangers. The horses helped by kicking the mangers apart. He finally managed to get the horses over to the other side of the barn, and into their own stalls, and the cows into the different places where they were supposed to be.

He gave the animals their feed in the proportions that his dad had described that morning, and got busy with hammer and nails. He was so busy for a while that he didn't have time to worry about where the Wampus Cat was. He needed to get the world back into order before his dad got home.

Later, when his dad did get home, he didn't bother telling him about everything that had happened.

It was funny how the Cat made that last ROAR sound something like a MOO. Was it trying to pass itself off as one of the herd while it was coming after Billy? Just like a wolf in sheep's clothing?

One thing was for sure, the animals had stampeded and were right behind Billy as he shot out of the woods. They were still right behind him as he was running across the open field toward the light. And they were still right behind him when he came flying through the barn door.

But what about that blackberry patch by the creek? Billy found a piece of his shirt hanging in the thorns the next day when he went out to round up the animals. And, what about all those scratches on his arms and back?

There was no doubt about it. The Cat had almost gotten him, and he had the claw marks to prove it!

Ever after that, Billy never needed to be reminded to not dawdle when he was supposed to be bringing the cattle in, and, especially, he didn't need to be reminded to get the animals in before dark.

What ever happened to the Wampus Cat?

According to Billy, "I have never seen one to this day, but I am certain that somewhere around Gnaw Bone, Indiana, there is a **Wampus Cat** lurking in the deep woods."

The author has thought about this for a long time. He went to a Cherokee family that lives near Gnaw Bone and asked them what they know about the warning the old-timer gave to Billy. They maintained that there actually is a Wampus Cat wandering where she chooses, and it's best to stay away from her as far as you can get.

Do you want to know more? Check out Wikipedia.

ABOUT THE AUTHOR

T he author lived on a farm just south of Gnaw Bone, Indiana in the 1940's and 1950's. He knew Billy Engel personally. The segments of this story reflect the culture of the times in this part of Indiana.

Conrad Reichert, Ph.D.

CPSIA information can be obtained
at www.ICGtesting.com
Printed in the USA
LVHW051325040121
675400LV00006B/1079

9 781630 507275